AN OCTOPUS HAS *THREE* HEARTS

GLYN ROBERTS

AN OCTOPUS HAS *THREE* HEARTS

A Collection of 10 Original Poems

By

GLYN ROBERTS

An Octopus Has *Three* Hearts

Copyright 2012 © Glyn Roberts

All rights reserved. No part of this publication may be reproduced, stored on a retrieval system, or transmitted, in any form or by any means, without permission of the author.

ISBN 978-1-4717-3680-3

CONTENTS

An Octopus Has *Three* Hearts 1
Unexploded Bomb 5
Paradise Mislaid 10
The Cowboy's Hat 13
Captain Scoundrel 19
Pretty White Mare 23
Inferno 28
Billy Liar 33
The Beautiful Land..............................37
Carry On Folking 40

Back from school, the young one asked, "Did you know, a jellyfish has no brain?"

I said... "Yes, I did." It was a fib, of course. But apparently they have no brain - jellyfish, that is. Kids have lots.

Then she said, "Well, did you know, an octopus has three hearts?"

"No," I said, "but I'm going to write a poem about it!"

And here's a poem about it...

An Octopus Has *Three* Hearts

An octopus was swimming the waters
of the Mediterranean sea
six arms were doing the backstroke
while two were in search of his tea,
for an octopus tastes with his arms
and uses them to hunt out his food
like shrimps and whelks and mussels
and whatever might suit his mood.

Now, as he groped in the water
a soft shape came to his touch
it was a *Sponge Bellied* jellyfish
that had swum by to give him a *cutch;*
she was graceful yet well rounded

with slim legs that could dance all night
so arms and legs were inseparable
for both, it was love at first sight.
But jellies, they are quite brainless
I mean, literally, they have no brain
so when a shark flashed his smile at her
she was gone, never seen again;
the octopus was broken hearted
but he still had another two
for an octopus has *three* hearts
so he got over her, with out more a do!

He swam on until he arrived
by a cave five fathoms down
he thought he'd have ten minutes peace
but a pair of eyes followed him round,
such pretty enticing orbs
the kind he'd never seen before
they gave a sexy, sideways stare
even though these eyes were on stalks.

It was a crab that crept up to the octopus
and she aimed to get her man
for she gripped with a pincer movement
to hug like a crustacean can;

it would have broken his bones, if he'd had any,

but he squirmed out of her grasp

then he came back to tickle her,

under her chin, and that made her gasp.

For a week or more they were happy

the octopus again was in love

till the crab waved her claws and snapped at him

and he realised, it was no good;

he propelled himself far away from her

though his heart was broken once more

but an octopus has *three* hearts

so he got over her, no problem, for sure!

Soon, he was away on the current

but then his mind turned to romance

and when a turtle swam toward him

he thought he might have a chance,

but the turtle was no push-over

she wouldn't, *turn turtle*, for him

not till they were better aquainted, she said,

so they just went out for a swim.

But then, as sometimes happens
on land and under the sea
creatures will fall for each other
(the wife says it once happened to me)
but the octopus and the turtle
soon were relaxing there in the surf
and as they lay on the beach together
they knew that they were in *lurve.*

Said the octopus to the turtle
"I trust that you will take care
of this here, last heart of mine
for after this, there isn't a spare!"
She said, "With me, you'll not be *heartless*
if you will please pardon the pun
and an octopus may have *three* hearts
but our two hearts, beat as one!"

Like a lot of cities, my home town of Manchester, was well blitzed in the Second World War. The Luftwaffe bombers arrived at the end of 1940 just in time for Christmas. Through the winter they dropped tons of high explosives and incendiaries to start as many fires as possible, just to keep everybody warm.

Now, although the war was great fun for some like the generals and kids out plane spotting, there were thousands of "Conchies" who didn't like fighting but did other war work including bomb disposal...

Unexploded Bomb

When Hitler bombed our chip shop
in 1941
he left an unexpected gift
in our street when he was done -
it wasn't wrapped, it had no card
not a clock, but it was ticking
"them nasty *Jermans* don't play fair
and need a damn good kicking!"

So said my Dad, to all us kids
down in the Anderson shelter
Mam just laughed and said our Dad
was all mouth and no trouser -
though like a mouse when the Sergeant called
with all that "call-up malarkey"

Dad wasn't scared to do his bit
just allergic to the khaki.

Old Trafford was left all a mess
worst bombs since the Christmas Blitz
even United's ground was kaput
all thanks to fiendish Fritz
and the flames still high, lit up the sky
like a Guy Fawkes night in Spring
to guide the bombers back next night
to have another fling.

Said PC Plodder to my Mam
"those Jerries won't let us be
take your young uns to a safer place
like your sister's, in Coventry"
but of course we wouldn't leave Dad behind
though officially he couldn't be found
that was our lie for nosey parkers
and the army, if they called round.

So, they cordoned off our terrace
and we had to leave for the day
up to Aunty Rose's house
for cake and lemonade

but I sneaked back to take a look
at the bomb left in our street
and at Dad behind the black out drapes
looking as white as a sheet.

Now this bomb probably weighed a ton
and was definitely as tall as me
and I was definitely the tallest
in the whole of Infant Three,
it stuck out the ground at an angle
and went *'tick, whirr, click'*
and oozed a kind of yellow muck
that reminded me of sick.

There were many busybodies
all peering at the bomb
before they found the need to go
to wherever they'd come from
but one lone figure stood there
he frowned then stroked his chin
next unscrewed the top of the bomb
and put his hand right in.

I think this bomb disposal chap
was the bravest I ever saw

as bold as Mister Churchill
when he started up this war
and as fearless as any man
fighting for our King
to mess with an unexploded bomb
must be a scary thing.

So I thought I'd go and have a word
when he'd had his cup of tea
ask how a Bomb Disposal Man
I might get to be
did you have to pass exams and stuff?
did it stop you going to fight?
that wouldn't be on, I thought,
for it was every Briton's right.

He just laughed when I told him this
said he wouldn't take up arms
"I couldn't kill another man
who's never done me harm"
but he would help his neighbours
at the risk of his own skin
to show them *warmongrels*
that war will never win.

He said he'd took the Peace Pledge,
though not where he'd took it to,
but he meant he was a *Patsy Fist*
and war would never do;
and thousands of men and women, he said,
weren't sure what the fighting's for
but would fight for common sense
and stand up against this war.

When everything had settled down
and we were safe indoors
I said to Dad, "You don't have to hide
there's lots to do in wars"
"You see, Son, I would," he said
"but my back is far too weak"
and Mam just laughed, "his back," she said,
"just has a yellow streak!"

This is my rewrite of Milton's epic poem "Paradise Lost" - well a bit of it anyway. The bit where Lucifer, who is God's favourite son is leaving home.

And God, like any proper parent, thinks it's his fault...

Paradise Mislaid

Young Lucifer was about to leave,
he said, "Look here, Dad,
you've been telling me I'm no good
since Adam were a lad
but I'll be *damned* if I agree
and accept that I'm all bad."

God, his father, was rather angry,
"Strewth! Help me someone
have I not given everything
to each and every son?
your place is here with your brothers
when all is said and done!"

But Lucifer was stubborn,
he said, "I need my own space,
where all that Goodness isn't
forever right in your face,
and what's more I've discovered

this amazing, *wicked* place!"

**Cried God, "Come here, Michael,
your young brother has gone quite mad
look, he's become *bedevilled*
by some rebellious fad
he's being so ungrateful
considering all he's had."**

**"Aye, and he's lazy," said Michael,
"though there's much work to do
we're building a heaven down on earth,
everything brand new;
us lads, we're all doing our best -
Lucifer should help out too!"**

**"Oh, really?" replied Lucifer,
"you're a bully as well
you lot can stay right here
I know where I'm off to dwell
you might want to serve in Heaven
but I will reign in Hell!"**

**"Don't go, Lucifer," pleaded God,
you're still my pride and joy**

**I've created all this life
but you just want to destroy
now get yourself back with us,
stop being a naughty boy!"**

**But by now it was far too late,
Lucifer was gone for sure
pals, Mammon and Be-elzebub
were waiting by the door
to welcome Lucifer into Hell,
his home for evermore.**

**For a while they chilled in Hell,
Lucifer without a care
but as there was little to do,
he had much time to spare
(this is before Human Sin,
so no souls to torment there.)**

**"I'll take a trip to Earth," he said,
"see what they did achieve
they built a paradise and garden,
so I'm led to believe
but while I'm there, I'll have some fun,
and check out this girl Eve...sssssssssssssss!"**

This is a poem about getting old, when even cowboys realise that one day they are boys no longer.

Or, as a wise philosopher (me) might have said, it's when an individual's needs no longer fit into the saddlebags of existence. Something like that, anyway...

The Cowboy's Hat

Old Jed was an old cowboy
he'd been cowboying for years
the oldest of all the cowboys
since a boy, he'd had this career,
up in the saddle at daybreak
riding the trail and the range
out in all weathers, was Jed,
in the sun and the wind and the rain.

Now a cowboy has few belongings
his horse, a gun and a knife
but for Jed his favourite possession
was the thing that might save his life,
it wasn't a spare bullet or bible,
a lucky charm or anything like that
it was made of rough stitched leather
and he wore it - it was his hat!

This hat was a tough kind of hombre
it was rigid and heavy as iron
and if the weather is bad in the winter
you need a hat to rely on
and under the hot sun of Texas
if you're lucky to tell the tale
a good hat is what might save you
from being white bones on the trail.

The trouble is (people will tell you)
what you're doing, never is right
and they were quick to tell old Jed
his hat looked such a fright,
surely he'd find much better
in the store in Witchita town
so just to be nice and friendly, like,
he decided to go and look round.

The store was one of those emporiums
that always has one of each thing
and over in the corner by a mirror
were the hats, new in for the Spring,
there was a comic villain's black stetson,
an alpine with feather in brim
a topper, an English billycock

and a straw boater with pink ribbon trim.

But the one that Jed cast his eye on
was sporty, modern and clean
it was a soft grey sombrero
and fitted old Jed like a dream,
said Jed, "I don't need you now,"
and flung down his old leather hat
then laughing to the storekeeper,
"You can do what you want with that!"

That Spring, old Jed was off trailing
herding the steers to the North
he was as happy as a cowboy called Larry
cowboying for all he was worth
and his new titfer well pleased him
for it was cool yet it was snug
and knowing that he was in fashion
he couldn't help but feel smug.

But always comes the winter,
***woooh...* them cold winds will blow**
across the plains of Kansas
followed by Ozark mountain snow,
Jed he borrowed an old scarf

**if you'd seen him you'd have laughed
he wound it around his sombrero –
it made him look right daft!**

**So he went and got a new hat
like those favoured by lumberjacks
and Jed became the first cowboy
with a peak and wool earflaps
and that summer he bought a visor
to keep the sun from his eye
then a cap with a cloth at the back
so that his neck might not fry.**

**There followed all sorts of headgear
Jed located along the trail
a Scotsman's tam-o-shanter
a Davy Crockett with fur tail
in Abilene he found a sou'wester,
why? Nobody could explain
and in Tulsa an Indian headdress
that was of little use in the rain.**

**Jed now had a saddle of headwear
that always fell out on the ground
he needed a home for them all**

was it time to settle down?
Maybe a spread, near Topeka
it had good grass he was told
with a rocker on the porch in the sunset,
"Darn, reckon I'm just getting old!"

In the past, Jed had all he needed
he would stop awhile in some place
part of the seasons and nature
then be gone and leave no trace,
he said, "I've got so fussy, now
and that's all there is to that
things used to be so simple
when I only needed one hat!"

On the Old Chisolm Trail by Wichita
Jed couldn't take any more
and went into the town emporium
the one he'd been in once before,
"I need a hat for all occasions
one that can do everything
whether in bed, in the saddle or dancing
from Summer through to the Spring."

The storekeeper smiled, then laughing,

"I don't think that hat could exist"
"But it did," replied old Jed, frowning,
and here, long ago, it was ditched."
"Wait, I might have something for ya,"
said the storekeeper and went out the back
he returned in a matter of minutes
holding a crusty, leather old hat.

He blew off the dust and he wiped it, said,
"I never did throw it away
there may be more choice in headwear
but you won't get this quality today."
Jed put on the hat and a tear came
"I've missed this old thing, you see"
the storekeeper grinned, "Then have it,
go on, please, take it for free!"

Here are some pantomime heroes and villains though not much to choose between them, as they are all as bloodthirsty as each other. This poem is ideal for children as it has flogging, hanging and murder, etc...

Captain Scoundrel

"Tremble all, run for your lives
I'm Captain Scoundrel at the wheel
your shining jewels will be my booty
all that's precious I will steal.

Every gold piece in this world,
if I had them all, I'd want more
for all you fools that hide your riches
be assured that death will call.

Open mouths on astonished faces
will splutter blood at my sword play
then dieing men will only whisper:
'Scoundrel took my life away!'

I am Scoundrel, a bloody pirate
who lives his life upon the waves
I care not for the love of people
but exploit their puny ways.

Many ship has fallen to me
and many men 'midst cries of pain
officers of powerful navies
cringe with fear at my curved blade.

Spanish sailors have begged for mercy
Englishmen have kissed my feet
all have had their hearts torn from them
and now are slumbering in the deep!"

* * *

"I'm Admiral Goody, the Navy's finest
I live for country, honour and creed
I'll take no rest till my mission's ended
to rid this Scoundrel from the sea.

They say he once killed a mermaid
a sacrifice to drink her blood
then raised his glass up to the Devil
in fiendish triumph over Good.

With God on my side I know I'll prosper
I kiss the Bible and salute the King
Hurrah! for the British Empire

'Rule Britannia,' we all will sing.

My duty is to those that pay me
protect the wealth that they once stole
but I'm not here to judge my betters
their admiration is my goal.

So, up with the rigging, splice the main brace
weigh the anchor and flog a man
I dare anyone to try and stop me
I'll have that Scoundrel, soon as I can.

For I don't fear him and his cutlass
I'll make him pay for his crimes
and have him swinging from the yardarm
then the glory will be mine!"

* * *

"My name is Vulture, the one *behind you*
as cannon blaze and steel cuts deep
the smashed in skulls and wicked faces
all that's left is mine to keep.

I have seen it, a thousand or more times

over the ages, always the same
cruel men as bad as each other
hurting and killing for money and fame.

Look; there is Scoundrel killing Goody
or is it the other way around?
Who cares, for whoever's the victor
I'll make sure he ends up drowned.

I'm always there, I'll be watching
until the final dying groan
when I move in amongst these madmen
to scrape the marrow from their bones.

I enjoy collecting eyeballs
pulling apart a broken spine
ripping the fat from dead men's bellies
all those that lived, now are mine.

For I'm the Vulture, the one who's waiting
and I'll be here till all is gone,
taking from fools and would-be heroes,
fools and heroes, but not for long!"

If read correctly, this next poem will give you a quick gallop upon the poem's eponymous four legged hero. Hang on to your hat! The names might be made up but the places are for real, around Dartmoor...

Pretty White Mare

A riderless pony returned to the stable
pretty white, pretty white, pretty white mare
the pony rode in but the saddle was bare
pretty white, pretty white mare.

Sir Henry Grimstone came to the stable
where was Margaret, his lady fair?
Thrown no doubt from out the saddle
left behind by the pretty white mare.

Sir Henry mounted the same white pony
rode that day, rode everywhere
though he went in each direction
couldn't find his Margaret anywhere.

"If I can find her I'll give her riches
offer her jewels beyond compare
a string of ponies which to ride upon
each one finer than the pretty white mare.

If I can save her I'll be a good man
and serve her always, I do swear
from today I'll bring her happiness
be more faithful than the pretty white mare."

He rode east, crossed the Walkham river
with no thought for his own welfare
would have drowned by being dragged under
if not for the skill of the pretty white mare.

He rode west into Wistman Forest
through a thicket that might ensnare
would have been torn by briar and hawthorn
but for the wits of the pretty white mare.

He rode north, he did not tarry
himself and the horse he would not spare
over miles of bog and peat hags
thanks to the strength of the pretty white mare.

He rode south and found a cavern
which he assumed was a wild beast's lair
then dismounted outside the entrance
and left behind the pretty white mare.

He went in with his heart a beating
on his lips a silent prayer
further into the cave he ventured
to see if his lady's bones were there.

But then he saw a young woman smiling
elated, it was his Margaret fair
but then he heard a young man laughing
and so he sank into despair.

"Lady, lady, why do you leave me
when I have endless wealth to spare?
Return with me to Grimstone Manor
and all I have is yours to share."

"What need I with all your money,
jewellery and your silverware
what do I want with all your riches?
For all your wealth the Devil may care!"

Up spoke the young man, "I am a bold one
thwart me and you'd best beware
I am now this lady's lover
cross swords with me, if you dare!"

Then up spoke Margaret in defiance
shaking back her golden hair
"Yes, I am now this young man's mistress
and he's my love, I do declare!

What's more, I want nothing from you
I even sent back my pretty white mare
to show my love for you has ended
of which you now must be aware. "

Up spoke Sir Henry, "I am your master
put an end to this affair
outside is the horse you speak of
return with me on the pretty white mare."

She said, "Of all you ever gave me
there is one thing I prize most rare
outside, is that which I speak of
will you return me, my pretty white mare?"

And so Sir Henry sadly relented
no wish to be reminded of his lady fair
then he took the young man's stallion
in exchange for the pretty white mare.

And so Lady Margaret kept her pony
pretty white, pretty white, pretty white mare
and never again would be parted from her
pretty white, pretty white mare.

Dante's "Divine Comedy" is a cracking allegorical vision of the wonders of Christian afterlife. In it, our hero, as a kind of spiritual tourist, journeys into Hell through its various layers, each worse than the last.

In the centre of Hell is a narky Satan (he's all tied up in chains) who is cleverly eating Judas's head and skinning his back at the same time! Great sense of humour, that Dante! Anyway, here's my version...

Inferno

Through a dark wood
basso loco, **deep place**
a man with sad eyes
below the sun's silent face
will cross River Acheron
hope sunk without trace
and weeping will walk
through Hell's lonely gate...

...and if you think that's bad
it gets worse, not better!
For mediaeval man
was such a miserable sinner
he would plead for forgiveness
to God, Jesus and the angels
he was a miserable *pleader*

in them miserable Middle Ages!

Dante says Hell has Nine Circles
each worse than the last
so he would have wanted
to hang about in the First
for the First is called Limbo
a second-rate Paradise
for deluded non-believers
and unbaptised good guys.

The Second Circle, is windswept
but it's not in simple gusts
for here you are exposed
to the warming winds of lust
you'll find here Achilles
and Cleopatra, the Egyptian lass
with a chance for some fun
and bad jokes about her - *asp.*

Now, Wales is known for weather
it once rained each day for a year
but Hell has rain that's frozen
that reaches up to your ears,
the Fourth Circle's there for misers

but also for the men of greed
they pull or push big boulders about
each according to his need.

It's Circle Five were now onto
where you swim in the River Styx
this river is so polluted
they should have called it the River Stinks,
fighting above, are the wrathful
drowning, are the slothful below
but a Jacuzzi party and sauna?
- a pleasure they'll never know.

In flaming tombs writhe heretics
who were probably burned on earth
so you'd think they'd be used to it
and blaze for all they're worth;
the Minotaur guards the violent
those violent in deed or word
and you don't mess around with a Minotaur,
least, that's what I've heard!

The sad ones are the suicides
their torment, in Hell, carries on
for now they are torn by thorns

as punishment for their *wrong*
and they are also clawed at by Harpies
with no reprieve or relief
for even after Judgment Day
they still will hang from the trees.

The Eighth Circle's for the malicious
the disloyal, frauds and thieves
so as we descend to Hell's centre
we find the cunning Ulysses
and all the blasphemers likewise
that offended the Christian way
but that was way in the past
and folk are more *tolerant* today.

The Ninth Circle traps the traitors
holds them forever in ice
Brutus betrayed poor Caesar
and now he pays the price
but Judas as you'd imagine
they save up the works for him
and here's where the lad himself, Satan,
here's where Satan comes in.

Yes! Finally Dante meets Satan

there in the middle of earth
and Satan is busy with Judas
torturing him for all he is worth
he's chewing on Judas's cranium
at the same time skinning his back
and as Hell will exist forever
it's ideal for a maniac!

Well, Dante is done with Inferno
but still there's more he must know
for his journey is not yet over
and he's got places to go
Purgatory next, then Paradise
soon he will be on his way
but those further adventures of Dante
is a poem for another day!

I did know someone called Joey McQueen once, but otherwise here is a pack of lies, innuendo and half truths, all a result of an excessive intake of alcohol which spills over on every third line of the poem...

Billy Liar

I had a half brother called Billy McQueen
he came in the Old Duke, I asked where he'd been
he ordered a drink, and after a think, said,
"Down by The Raffles Club, guess what I seen?"

Now Billy tells stories you take with some salt,
from a family of liars it's hardly his fault
he stared at his beer, said, "Now listen here,
I think I've been witness to a *spooky* assault."

"What happened Billy?" we wanted to know
"Who was it this time, who gave the blow?"
he picked up his glass, "It was a young lass," he said,
"She smacked John the Bouncer right on the nose!"

Some shook their heads at this sign of the times

where no one's safe from such violent crimes

Bill drained the last drop, and said, "But guess what?

John got up, and then he just smiled."

We couldn't believe it - a bouncer amused?

the knock to his nose must have left him confused

Bill with fresh ale, continued his tale, said,

"No! John was happy, though he'd just been abused."

"You see, he said he'd found Jesus, one night on the door,

he was searching for knives but got something more"

Bill rolled up a cig, then took a swig, and said,

"Our John is a different bouncer for sure."

"Has he got a halo, or grown wings?" someone sniggered

"Can he do miracles?" said another, then shivered

"You might take the piss, but I tell you all this,

he was turning his cheek, that's what I figure."

By now Billy was drunk and rambling on
about God and religion and where it went wrong
he held up a gin, yelled, "Here's to sin!"
then quickly downed his next beer in one.

"Who's for The Raffles?" we then heard him shout,
"Let's have a session, a bit of a bout
we might see the light if we're bladdered tonight
and even St. Peter can't keep us out!"

So we staggered to The Raffles, and yes, it was so
for John's broken nose had a heavenly glow
he urged, "Let in Christ, tonight drinks are half price,
and I'll watch over till it's your time to go."

Now a bouncer's a hard man and looks to himself
but there could be a time he needs something else
it might be booze, for some it's drugs they choose

I guess John looked within for some spiritual help.

So Billy had told the truth, perhaps his story inspires
for a thoughtful bouncer is one to admire
so when next in the bar, Billy, I'll buy you a jar
and sorry, our kid, if I called you a liar.

Imagine a foreboding sky, wind swept moors, a dark valley, cramped terraced houses clinging to a hillside and a forlorn graveyard in November...well, that's the advert for where I live, here's the poem...

The Beautiful Land

Miss Chapel buried her mother
and so he put on the black armband
"My condolences to you, Miss Chapel
it was a peaceful end, I understand"
"Thank you, Mr. Bob, mother's gone now
to that promised, beautiful land
you see, she was Jehovah's witness
and waiting to dwell at Jesus' right hand.

"Miss Chapel, may I offer,
I don't believe, but as a young man
I got a likeness of that, there Jesus
a tattoo, imagine if you can,
upon a cross, across my shoulders
and there, for all my life, he'll hang
I never, ever, was religious but...
played guitar in a heavy metal band!"

Miss Chapel wept by the graveside

of her mother, now gone to rest
"My sympathies to you, Miss Chapel
but perhaps it's all for the best"
"Thank you Mr. Bob, yes, mother's gone now
and by me she will be missed
but you see she was a believer
and waiting to meet with Heaven's blessed."

"Miss Chapel, may I offer,
I hope you don't think I'm in jest
only in films do the dead walk again
and where we go is anyone's guess
Heaven and Hell, to me, mean nothing
though as a young man, I must confess...
I got tattoos of skulls with wings
and the words 'Hell's Angels' across my chest!"

Miss Chapel was all alone now
in her gloomy house upon the hill
"My greetings to you, Miss Chapel
you no longer need your nursing skill"
"Yes, Mr. Bob, mother's gone now
for too many years she was ill
and now my life has little purpose
though mother's presence is with me still."

"Miss Chapel, may I offer,
to protect you from that eerie chill
it's time for us to be together
we've dwelt on death but have had our fill
we'll put the past where it belongs, behind us
where it won't control against our will
the dead are dead and life's for living
and at our age we've no time to kill!"

There's an old folk song that goes:

"Soldier, oh soldier, won't you marry me, with your musket, fife and drum?

Oh no, pretty maid, I cannot marry you, for I have a wife of my own"

I wrote this folk poem for Frankie Howard and would have sent it to him but alas he is gone, ooer...

Carry On Folking

"Baker, oh baker, will you marry me
I've a bun in the oven you plainly can see
it happened that one time when you *kneaded* me
will you be my husband so we can be three?"

"Pretty young Miss you're a blossoming *flour*
don't take it amiss and think I am *sour*
***dough* I once loved you I've my own wife instead**
and very soon now we will have *bred!"*

"Farmer, oh farmer, will you marry me
I've grown round the middle you clearly can see
it happened that one time you fertilised me
will you be my husband so we can be three?"

"Pretty young Miss we rolled in the hay
don't take it amiss if I stay a *whey*
it *o curd* to me to now share my home
so I married another, my oats I have sown!"

"Sailor, oh sailor, will you marry me
I'm now up the tub you boldly can see
it happened that one time you Jolly Rogered me
will you be my husband so we can be three?"

"Pretty young Miss you are a *meremaid*
don't take it amiss if I seem afraid
I won't come about, like a fish to be caught
I've my own wife, besides, well, one in each port!"

"Sergeant, oh Sergeant, will you marry me
I've got into trouble it's evident to see
it happened that one time you went and frisked me
will you be my husband so we can be three?"

"Pretty young Miss now *police* listen hear
don't take it amiss if I don't come near
you whetted my whistle one day in my life

but my truncheon's now only there for my wife!"

"Blacksmith, oh Blacksmith, will you marry me
I'm all banged up as *shoe* can see
it happened that one time you went and stoked me
will you be my husband so we can be three?"

"Pretty young Miss I poked up your fire
don't take it amiss and think me a liar
but I've *metal* the woman I now want to meet
I have my own wife and she can't be beat!"

"Butcher, oh butcher, will you marry me
I've now got a pudding, I'm stuffed can't you see
it happened that one time you filleted me
will you be my husband so we can be three?"

"Pretty young Miss, yes, I porked your pie
don't take it amiss if I now don't come by
we can't *beef* friends, I *veal* I can't cheat
I've a wife of my own, you and I *mutton meat!"*

"Vicar, oh vicar, will you marry me

I confess I am pregnant you *holy* can see

it happened that one time you had communion with me

will you be my husband so we can be three?"

"Pretty young Miss I do hear your prayer

don't take it amiss and think me unfair

we must bear our burden, we reap what we sow

and so says my wife and God, she should know!"

"Soldier, oh soldier, will you marry me

I've a tum like a drum and all down to thee

it happened that one time you beat rhythm with me

will you be my husband so we can be three?"

"Pretty young Miss I *musket* away

don't take it amiss if I do not stay

if *fife* misled you, you know it's well known

soldiers in folksongs have wives of their own!"

www.ingramcontent.com/pod-product-compliance
Ingram Content Group UK Ltd.
Pitfield, Milton Keynes, MK11 3LW, UK
UKHW021051270726
13967UKWH00012B/278

9 781471 736803